# 5 Pillars For The Ideal Lifestyle Of The Construction Company Owner

John Bergman

# Acknowledgments

There are so many people to thank that I have gotten to know over the last 25 years that it would be difficult to list them all here. Construction company owners are a great bunch of people providing services and projects that are very important to the economy in general and to their customers in particular.

In addition to the contractors I've been privileged to work with, there are many consultants that have worked with me building the reputation I'm proud of. We all agreed on the core philosophy that guided the company. We were committed to bringing value to every client and always put the client's needs ahead of our own. When value drives your company you can't go wrong.

Special thanks to Kim Lee Harden, who was my senior consultant through the years and the person I leaned on when there was a question on how to get the job done. I always knew that when Lee guided a project, the customer would get the results they were looking for. Many clients wrote to me to tell me how happy they were with the work that Lee performed.

## About the Author

Allow me to start this book by telling you I am not a contractor, although I have had the opportunity for about twenty five years to work with and coach hundreds of contractors, both large and small. I have worked with general contractors and every trade in the business, from concrete, to framing, to roofing, etc.

I have been around the block, and one thing I have learned is that often, contractors start their business for all the wrong reasons and, therefore, start off on the wrong foot. They create a job, rather than a business, and they don't understand why they're working twelve hours a day, seven days a week, for less money than they were making when they were drawing a pay check. It's hard for many to know how to separate their business from their life.

My job has always been to help bring sanity to an insane business and to teach contractors how to work as a business owner and work on their business, instead of spending all their time, working in their business. As a contractor, your business is separate from your life. You can be a successful construction company owner and still have a life away from the business.

I couldn't tell you how to do the technical side of the business, such as framing a house, pouring a driveway, or putting a roof on a house. I am not qualified to do that. What I have been able to do is help contractors learn to transform their company into a stable, thriving business without giving up the rest of their life.

What I will be sharing with you over the next several pages of this small book are things I have learned and I have taught contractors that have helped them transform and grow their businesses while maintaining a healthy lifestyle. I have helped contractors change from small businesses, where the owner is buried in the day to day details of the business, to one where the owner can work on the business, instead of in it. You can be home for dinner on a regular basis, attend your children's important events, and take a long vacation, without fear of loss.

One of my clients grew his business from six million dollars to sixty million dollars, because we put in the systems that were necessary to run the business, without his having to be involved in every aspect of the business. In addition, he was active in off road racing several time a year while he grew his business. That should be your goal.

When I first met him, he said that every time he tried to grow his business, his margins shrank, so he decided to just stay at $6 million in revenue and forget more growth. Once we showed him how to manage the business, without his day to day involvement with all details, things changed dramatically. All of a sudden he was able to grow the business while maintaining an active lifestyle with his hobbies and family.

Over the years, I have seen contractors lose their homes; lose their families because of the demands of the business. I've seen them watch their money disappear, because someone they trusted embezzled the money. Often, it was a girlfriend, who also worked as their accountant. That happened, because they were too busy working in the field and had little knowledge of the accounting system. That's not the way you want to run your business.

As you read this book, I will be laying out strategies for how to plan your business, how to develop systems that will control your business, how to make sure the way you bid a project is the way a project comes in, so you protect your margins. In addition, you will have the tools to track the flow of money, both in and out of the business.

By the time you get through with this book, you will have learned a great deal about how to run your business without giving up the rest of your life, again, not from a technical aspect, such as framing, pouring concrete, etc., but from a business point of view. I want you to turn your business into the Ideal Construction Company and to have a business that works for you, rather than you working for the business. Your business should support your life and your lifestyle.

Your goal should be to have a business that will run without you. You should be able to walk out the door for two, three weeks, a month, and know the business will continue to run, even though you are not there. That's the ultimate goal. It's only then that you've created something of value that you could pass on to your children or sell to another contractor. You have created equity; you've created an asset with real value.

If the business depends totally upon you, people can't buy you, and they don't want to buy you. They want to buy a running, functioning business, and the only way to do that is to change your thinking and do your planning to develop your systems, so the business will run without your day-to-day involvement. In that way, you've not only created an asset, but a lifestyle that serves you well.

## One Contractors Story

*The Road to Success Comes from Hard Work, Determination, and Sacrifice...*while the author of this quote certainly had the best intentions of expressing the characteristics of any business owner, I feel that it falls far short of what is truly needed to be successful at any business, much less a construction company. What should be added is ...Tenacity, Education, Opportunity, Connections, Loyal Staff, and......A Plan!

The proverb "Necessity is the Mother of Invention" has never been more true of how I came to be my own boss. My partner and I started our small business 30 years ago in the bedroom of our house as a means to address the important things in life...namely, food and shelter. We had no money, no business experience, no college degrees, and frankly no prospects for success. My partner had field experience, I knew what went on in an office and how to type. Beyond these basics, the only other things we had in our favor was determination, tenacity, and an absolute lack of fear of hard work. When your basic survival is at stake, you will be surprised at what you can accomplish.

Throughout the years, I always attributed any hardships we faced to our lack of formal education. I anxiously awaited my son's college graduation with a degree in Business Administration as a means to gain all the knowledge which I had missed by dropping out of college myself. Then I realized...education wasn't going to magically solve all the problems either. Sometimes experience trumps education.

As the years progressed, I slowly began to realize that opportunities come and go, connections are beneficial, but can only contribute to a certain point. We had a wonderful, loyal staff, but never had we ever developed a "Plan" for success. I set hard to work reading everything I could get my hands on, attending all types of seminars, webinars, and trying to fill the gaps in my knowledge in hopes that I could develop this mysterious "Plan" on my own. I learned about business plans, succession plans, various lofty economic theories, business concepts, Lean, Six Sigma, marketing approaches, you name it, I've probably gained at least a basic understanding of it all, but most of it didn't quite fit. Plan? From what I had read, "plans" were for huge corporations that had tons of money to spend on coaches, marketing departments, and highly paid executives with master's degrees and decades of experience at running a business.

Like most companies our size, and particularly our background, we had moved through more than a decade with no clear direction on where we wanted to take our business. We showed up for work, took care of what needed to be done, and repeated it all the next day. We didn't have written job descriptions, a written business plan, or a succession plan, and frankly, I don't think that when we started the business that we really had any "plan" that we would succeed at all, but somehow, we had done just that; in spite of ourselves.

Our business continued to grow and the chaos grew right along with the sales. There came a time when my partner and I realized we had to get things under control and we needed help. We decided to look for a business coach. Armed now with experience, a true understanding of the areas in which we needed help, and a determination to gain all that we could from an expert, we set out to find an individual who could provide true assistance and real direction. Our search led to John Bergman.

John worked tirelessly with us to get the upper hand on the chaos and prepare our "plan". As it turned out, there wasn't just one, but several; each complementing the other towards the overall goal of building a stronger foundation for our business for the future. The book you now hold in your hand is one of the most concise, clearly written "road maps" for your small construction business. It contains real information that you can implement directly and immediately; providing explanations and examples that are easy to understand and adapt to your specific needs. Make the time to develop your "plans" and work tirelessly to refine and expand it as you grow your business. Start small, revisit the plans often, and expand as you grow. I can tell you from experience that it is much easier to go forward from an initial plan than it is to try to reach back ten years and undo the mistakes that you will make without at least a framework of your goals.

## Table of Contents

Introduction ................................................................................... 1

Chapter One – The Ideal Construction Company ................... 7

Chapter Two - Pillar One – Intention ......................................... 15

Chapter Three - Pillar Two - Vision ............................................. 22

Chapter Four - Pillar Three – Planning ....................................... 26

Chapter Five - Pillar Four – Organize .......................................... 44

Chapter Six - Pillar Five – Building Your Systems ..................... 65

Chapter Seven – Know Your Numbers ....................................... 73

Chapter Eight – Performance Management ............................. 86

Getting Started .............................................................................. 93

# Introduction

Is your business serving your ideal lifestyle, or are you serving your business? Are you working for your business or is your business working for you? If your business isn't providing the lifestyle you want, you need to rethink your business and make changes.

**Ideal Lifestyle**

Since this book is about creating the ideal lifestyle, **"What is an ideal lifestyle?"** What's ideal for me may differ totally from what would be ideal for you. Let me pose a few questions to get your juices flowing:

- Could you walk out of your business today and go on a month-long vacation, knowing that when you come back, your business will be stable, profitable, and growing?

- Was your business designed from the beginning to become independent and run and grow successfully without you?

- Are you able to be home for family dinner time most days?

- Are you able to attend all or most of your children's important events, such as games, recitals, etc.?

- Are you able to separate your business life from your personal life?

- Would you say you have the ideal lifestyle that allows you to enjoy your family, your hobbies, etc.?

I'm sure you could add to this list, but you get the idea. When your business depends totally or mostly on you being there, managing every project to meet your margins, it interferes with your lifestyle.

It's been my observation over the past 25 years that most small construction company owners work far too many hours for the money they earn, the risk they take, and the sacrifices they make. The simple reason for that is that most owners are really technicians, not business people. Most have had little, if any, training on how to organize and run a business, so they suffer with too much stress, too much work.

If the business depends totally on you being there, making sure everything gets done and your projects come in on time and on budget, you've got a problem. You have no business, you have a job, and you're working for a lunatic. You may have started your company, so you had no boss looking over your shoulder, but guess what? You now have more bosses looking over your shoulder, including your customers, your vendors, your banker, and your employees, each with their own demands.

There is a better way to build a construction company, if you're willing to step back and look at a bigger picture. Put on your entrepreneur hat, and let's build your business the correct way, so you can have the life you dreamed of.

In this book, I will outline a 5 step program that will show you how to have a successful construction company, without giving up the rest of your life. I hope you picked up this book, looking for answers, and you're open to learning a better way.

## An Independent Business

For several reasons, you should design your business to run independent of you. That doesn't mean you should have no involvement, but you should be able to take a month's vacation and know that, when you get back, your business would not have missed a beat. You should be able to have the lifestyle you want, spending more time with the family, spending more time with your hobbies, or whatever you desire.

Having a business independent of you doesn't happen by accident. It has to be your **intention** and your purpose. **Intention is the first pillar**, which you will soon learn. The best time to design your business to be independent is before you open your doors for business. Most of my clients for the past 25 years have been in business over 20 years, so it requires a little restructuring.

Another important reason to design your business to be independent of you is for an exit strategy. A business dependent on the owner has little value. A business with a solid foundation that will run independent of the owner has much more value. You can't buy the owner, but you can buy a functioning business. I've seen more owners who had invested 20 or 30 years just liquidate their business to retire. How much better it would have been had they done their planning to increase the value of their business!

**An independent business requires systems and controls:**

There should not be a function of the business you don't understand. That doesn't mean you have to be there, but have systems with checks and balances that keep you informed.

There's another issue if you're spending most of your time in the field, depending on someone else to run your office and accounting.

**THEFT!**

I recently had lunch with a client and was told his trusted assistant had managed to steal $515,000 from him over the past 3 ½ years. She had been with the company for 13 years and was thought of as part of the family. How sad is that? Had he had the systems with checks and balances in place, this would not have happened.

Another contractor told me his trusted assistant, who was also his girlfriend, embezzled more than $200,000. What makes this interesting is that I was referred to him by one of my clients. We met, and he said he definitely wanted us to help him improve his business. His girlfriend told him that if he hired us, she would quit. That should have been a red flag, but it wasn't. The rest, as they say, is history.

There are so many potential problems when your business isn't designed to run without you; it makes no sense not to strive to make it so. Having the systems in place that help you accomplish that is not rocket science. **It simply takes the intention to do so.**

**A key person leaves:**

When you don't have operational systems in place, detailing how a job or function is done, you're vulnerable.

Another client I was referred to lost his office assistant, who also did his accounting. She got mad at her work load and simply called him, while he was on a job, to tell him she quit. She felt the demands put on her were too much for what she was paid, and she left without notice. She indicated she had tried to talk to him, but he was always too busy.

When he got back to the office, later that day, he realized he had no clue what she did or how she did it. She had done the accounting, billing, collections, scheduling, etc. He tried calling her home, but got no answer. When he went through her desk, he found unopened mail with demands for payment from vendors, and even some checks not deposited.

He now had a new job, figuring out how to do her job and finding a replacement. Being a trooper, he decided he could work in the field during the day and work in the office at night, straightening things out. What's wrong with this picture?

Too often, we find owners without proper systems in place, which leaves them vulnerable in several ways. If you have systems detailing the key positions, at least, you will not be left high and dry, and it will be easier to bring someone in and train them in the position.

**Find a balance:**

You can go overboard with systems and strangle your company by micromanaging. You want to have systems that give you standards on how a job is done, but you don't want to kill initiative. If your employees have suggestions for improving a system, listen and consider.

I had a client who got so caught up with systems, he went overboard and put systems in everything. When employees pushed back, he asked me to come in and do another analysis of the business. It turned out that he was holding on too tight and choking the business. He had become the problem by going overboard with too many systems.

I recommended he get rid of some systems he had put in place, and things improved almost immediately. There are operational systems that help and those that strangle the business. Knowing the difference is the key to success.

**Set a goal to create the Ideal Construction Company?**

## Chapter One – The Ideal Construction Company

I've been a business coach/consultant for more than 25 years, and I can tell you that you can build the **Ideal Construction Company** with a change in your mindset and the willingness to go to work **ON** your business, instead of **IN** your business. It isn't difficult if you are open to change and are willing to think outside the box.

In this book, I will show you 5 Simple Steps to Building the Ideal Construction Company by planning and building operational systems that produce consistent results on every project you do. Do it the MacDonald's way. Ray Croc could franchise his company around the world, in such a way, he could put teenagers in charge and produce the same product, no matter where you went. It resulted from planning and building operational systems. You aren't making hamburgers, but you can accomplish the same thing.

Instead of thinking of yourself as a contractor and the technical side of what you do, you need to ask yourself how to think as a business owner. Expand your thinking to the **business** of contracting, instead of the **work** of contracting. In that way, we can build or rebuild your construction business, so it works every time with consistent results. Only when you think of your company as a business, instead of a place to go to work, will you be able to make the transition necessary to build the Ideal Construction Company.

When I ask contractors what a Ideal Construction Company would look like, I get different answers. I'm usually told there is no such thing as a Ideal Construction Company. I would suggest the reason owners feel that way is because they are used to doing business like everyone else and can visualize nothing else.

The simple answer to what a Ideal Construction Company is would be one that produces consistent results, without the owner having to give up the rest of his or her life. It could function well, without the owner having to manage every aspect. It could run smoothly, without the owner being present. The owner would have time to work **ON** the business, instead of working **IN** the business and have a full life outside the business.

This will happen when the owner or owners have taken the time to do the planning and build the operational systems to run the business as a business, instead of a job to go to. Only a handful have reached this point in their development. My job is to help owners transform their company, so it realizes its full potential, without the owner working longer hours for less pay than having a regular job.

My next question is, what are the most important functions in a Ideal Construction Company? Here again, I get many answers, but the two most frequent are **project management and estimating.** Other answers include accountability and your employees. While all of those are important ingredients, they are not the answer. The answer is planning and operational systems that clarify and guide every function of the company.

Most construction firms get started by one person, who is tired of working for another company and believes they can make more money on their own and have more control over their time. They are good at what they do and running a business can't be that difficult.

Let me introduce you to Frank. Frank is a typical contractor with that entrepreneurial urge to own his own business.

**Frank's Construction Company**

Frank studied at night for his contractor's license, and now that he has it, he is ready to make the leap. Frank was offered a small project by a friend, so Frank's Construction Company is setup to offer remodeling and home building. Frank took out a loan to tide them over and set up shop at home. His wife loved him and wanted to give him support, even though she wasn't sure it was a good idea.

At this point, Frank is doing all the work, but that's okay, because he's his own boss, and he gets all the profit. He puts in his time and goes home at night happy that he has his own business. What he has is a job, not a business, but he hasn't realized that yet. That will come later, as he gets more projects.

Frank knows he has to have more projects, so he advertises in the penny saver, Craig's list, and the church bulletin. He's been involved in the church for several years, so he is well known. Even before he finished his first project, he gets a second and then a third. At this point, there was a lot of work available, so Frank looked for experienced contractors he could hire. He recognized that he couldn't keep running the company out of his home, so he rented a small office.

Known for the quality of work he provided, he had a backlog of work ahead of him. He hired 3 contractors and a young girl, Jane, to answer the phone and, more or less, run the office. He spent more time on the phone looking for work and answering complaints from customers who weren't happy with the work his employees were doing. He ran from job to job, trying to make things right. He had hired experienced contractors, assuming they would produce the same quality of work he did. **Big Mistake!**

Besides all of that, he also had to look for more work to keep everyone busy, do the estimating, collect the money, do payroll, go to the bank, and handle piles of paperwork pertaining to the business he had never done. He was spending much more time at work, and his family life suffered. If he had a bad day, that came home with him. He would even get calls at home from unhappy customers.

Running a business was far more complicated than the job he left. Is this what he wanted? He thought running his own business would be a lot more fun and give him more time with the family and the things he wanted to do.

A few months later, he had to hire more contractors due to the increase in business. His problems grew exponentially. He hired a bookkeeper, Bob, to help him keep track of the money. By this time, he had 12 employees, and the demands on his time were growing. He began leaving home earlier and coming home later. He rarely had time for his children, and his marriage was strained. His wife just didn't understand the pressure and stress he was under.

Money became a major issue for Frank. He found out that collecting money was harder than he thought it would be, so he had gone into debt, using his home as collateral for the loan. That gave him a cushion, but he still had the problem of making payroll each week and keeping up with his suppliers. Often, he was the last to get paid and, sometimes, there simply wasn't enough money for him. When he worked for someone else, he got a weekly paycheck. Now, he often doesn't. Still, Frank thought if he just worked harder, he could pull through this period and things would improve. He had plenty of work ahead of him, so he just needed to apply himself.

His bookkeeper, Bob, couldn't seem to provide Frank with a good financial picture of the firm, so Frank knew for sure how much money he had to work with. Bob was also supposed to keep track of what was owed to the company and try to collect it. Unfortunately, Bob was not very good at collecting money, so Frank had to do most of the collecting from difficult customers. Frank was afraid to put too much pressure on Bob for fear that Bob would leave and Frank would then have to do the bookkeeping.

Suddenly, Jane called Frank on one of the jobs he was checking on and announced that she was quitting that day. She felt over loaded and unappreciated for the work she had to do. Unfortunately, Frank had no clue what Jane did, so he did not understand that she was overloaded. By the time Frank got back to the office, Jane had gone. He found a note telling him where to mail her check that was due that week. He tried often to call Jane at home, but there was no answer.

A real sense of panic set in, when he realized he knew nothing about what Jane did or how to run the office on top of everything else. The phone kept ringing, and his contractors were calling his cell phone for instructions on what they should do. He took a deep breath and decided he would work in the office that night to get a sense of what he needed to do.

That night, he sat down and went through Jane's desk. What he found shocked him beyond belief. He found checks that had not been opened or deposited, invoices from suppliers that were overdue, and some threatened to put him on COD if he couldn't bring his accounts up to date. A renewal for his contractor's license was almost past due.

It appeared that Jane had not been doing the job she should have been doing. Then it occurred to Frank he had been too busy to give her good guidance or instructions and wasn't even sure what she should do. She had worked for a contractor before, so he assumed she would know what needed to be done. Like he did with the contractors he hired, he took her on faith she knew what to do.

So here was Frank; his business in shambles and his marriage on the rocks. He started with such great hope and confidence. What went wrong? Does any of this sound familiar? It's surprising that I have worked with companies that have been in business for 20 years or more that are suffering with some of the same problems. Mainly, the owner is so busy doing it, doing it, doing it in the field that they have little time to manage their business.

**Where did things go wrong for Frank?**

The interesting thing is that things went wrong, right from the beginning. Had Frank and his wife sat down and planned the business beyond the technical side, they may not have wound up with the mess that resulted with Frank on overload and his business and marriage on life support.

Every business should start with a **Strategic Business Plan and Operational Systems**. Your plan will lay out your vision, your purpose, who you will serve, and how you will serve them. Lay out a plan for who you will hire and what skills they should have. Every job should have a clear job description or position guide that clarifies what is expected of them. That means, you need to start with an understanding of what each job entails from the beginning.

Your operational systems will spell out not only what you want done, but how you want it done. This eliminates any confusion with your employees and gives you the foundation for hiring and training new employees. If someone suddenly leaves, as Jane did, it isn't a catastrophe, because you can bring someone in and get them up to speed quickly. I've seen contractors do video tapes on various parts of the job, showing exactly how they want it done. This is not nearly as daunting a task as you may imagine.

You need to have a clear understanding about money and how it flows through your business. Money is critical for any business, but it is especially true for contractors. That's because the time between completing a job and getting paid for the job can, sometimes, stretch out for 60-90 days or more. You still must meet payroll and your overhead expenses before you get paid. That means, you have to have a clear picture of your cash flow and expenses for at least the next 6 weeks. Without cash flow, a business can die, even if it shows a profit on paper.

You need to understand the difference between income and profit. Income is paid to the contractor when the job is done. Profit is what is left over after all expenses have been paid. Job cost every job, so you can see whether you're making a profit on each job. That way, you can tell what you're doing well and what you aren't. It may also show you that you shouldn't be doing that type of work. I will get into the financial side of the contractor's business in a later chapter.

For now, let's begin by looking at the Five Pillars.

## Chapter Two - Pillar One – Intention

I've been asked why I chose 5 Pillars, instead of 5 Steps, or 5 Ideas, etc. The reason is that pillars support a structure, such as a roof. Pillars will support your business in its transformation.

**Intention**

The first and most important pillar is your **intention.** If you aren't fully committed, intending to make your business independent of you, then you may not want to start down this path. It will take a strong commitment, because it is a significant change in the way you've been doing your business.

It takes three types of people to run a business, a technician, a manager, and an entrepreneur. The technician does things; the manager organizes things, and the entrepreneur has the vision to grow the business. Most owners are technicians and more prone to getting things done. Some can also manage and organize, but very few are entrepreneurs.

If you are an owner, who is more of the technician spending most of your time in the field, getting things done, this will be a major transition for you. You will have to change the way you see your business and be solidly committed to making the changes necessary.

**The Technician**

Most owners I've met over the past 25 years are technicians at heart. Many have grown their business, but often, it was due to market conditions, not great planning. Many have a business in chaos, repeating the same mistakes over and over again, because they have not figured out how to move to the entrepreneur phase.

Chances are that when you started your business, it wasn't with the idea of growing a business. You were just trying to create a job, a place to go to work and earn a living. You weren't thinking about growth; that was the last thing you wanted. You were comfortable working in the field, on projects away from a boss telling you what to do.

You were finally free to do what you wanted to do. The hours you worked were no problem, because you were your own boss, and you would do whatever it took to be your own boss. Doing what you want and staying in your comfort zone, focusing on the work, is what dooms the business. You'll never move until you change your mindset.

There's nothing wrong with being the technician, doing the work, if that is all you want, but it is a trap. At this point, you and your business are the same. If you were removed from the business, there would be no business, because you are the business.

In the technician stage, you are doing what you know how to do, and you do it well. Chances are that, because you are good at what you do, you will get more work, and the business will grow. It will be too much for one person, so you hire another person to help you. Now, there are two of you to keep busy, so you now have to look for and sell more work, supervise the work, bill and collect for the work done, etc.

At this point, you have to be a master juggler, doing things you didn't know how to do. Suddenly, you find you are dropping the ball, and some things aren't getting done. Trying not to panic, you realize the business is growing and changing. All you wanted to do was to create a job, but you are getting referrals from happy customers, and you're getting overloaded. You feel a combination of pride and panic and wonder how to handle it all.

As time goes on, your business grows because of your reputation, and you now have 5 employees in the field, and you hire your first office manager. You need someone to answer the phone, do the accounting, billing, collecting, banking, etc. You've never done those jobs and really don't want to, so you look for someone with experience and hope they are as good as they say they are.

You're still the technician and part-time manager of your people in the field. The office is another matter, because you have no experience with that side of the business. Things seem to get out of control, and you find it hard to keep up. You decide that, if you just work harder and longer, you can make this work. You work 12 hours a day, then 14 hours a day, and then there aren't enough hours in the day.

You finally reach that hard decision, when you admit the business can't keep going this way. It's time either to lock the doors and move on or make changes, but how? You're already working all you can, and you can't keep up. You started your business to get away from the boss, and now, you realize that your business is the boss.

The business doesn't work for you; you work for your business, and it has become a very demanding boss. All you wanted was to do the work you love, but now, you are doing everything else, trying to keep afloat. If all you want is to do the work you love, then you should shut the business down and go to work for someone else doing the work you love or keep the business small, just enough work for you.

There's nothing wrong with being the technician; it's only wrong when you're the technician and business owner, because you are focused on the tactical side of the business, instead of the strategic side, which is the entrepreneurial side that will allow you to create the lifestyle you wanted in the first place.

Clients have often said, "My customers rely on me and expect me to be on the job. If I'm not on the job, I may not get the business." I've heard that often and have proven you can train your customers to rely on your staff, not you, personally. That means you have to have the staff and the operational controls that will produce the results your customers expect.

Another thing I've heard is, "I make more money when I run the projects." That's probably true, but is it because you haven't trained your people correctly or you don't have the operational controls you should have? The other thing to consider is what your life and health is worth. Is it really worth working the way you do for a little extra profit?

As long as your business and your customers depend on you being there, your business will not mature and reach its full potential. If your customers are depending on you being there, they aren't buying what your business can deliver; they're buying what you can deliver. You will be trapped with a job that will demand too much and give you less than you deserve.

The purpose of starting a business is to get free of your boss and your job. Trading the boss you left for the boss you have now makes little sense. You need to focus on how to build a business that will provide jobs for other people and the lifestyle you want. You can't do that when you're a technician, instead of an entrepreneur. You can't simply ignore the roles of manager and entrepreneur, just because you don't understand them, if you want a successful business.

So now, you're at the crossroads. You can go back to being small, you can close the doors, or you can go for broke and try to survive. That means you have to throw everything into your business and be there all the time. There goes the rest of your life and possibly your family. Is that what you want?

Getting small again is the natural reaction to the pain of being out of control and out of your comfort zone. It's the resistance to learning what you need to do to become an entrepreneur, prepared to learn how to facilitate the growth of your business in a healthy and balanced way.

This is the point where you have to do soul searching and ask yourself if you're ready to learn what it will take to grow your business in a responsible way. Decide if you have a strong intention to turn your business into a mature business that can, ultimately, run without you. More than intention, it requires passion to do so.

Growth will bring additional responsibilities, require new skills and capital, and require a commitment well beyond that of the technician. The good news is; you can learn how to become the entrepreneurial business owner you need to be if you're committed to do so.

**Cutting the Umbilical Cord**

If you've cut the umbilical cord and changed your business, so it no longer depends on you, you will have to decide what you really want from your business and how it will serve your life. **Begin with the end in mind.**

When Tom Watson started IBM, he began by thinking about what the company would look like when it was done. How would it have to act? What would it have to be like? Once he made those decisions, he built the company to meet that vision. He was quoted as saying, "We didn't do business at IBM, we built one. He had no passion for doing the business; he had a passion for the business, itself.

Most business owners don't start with a model of a business that works, but rather, with the work to be done. The entrepreneur thinks about how the business must work; the technician focuses on how the work must be done. Do you see the difference?

If you've been in business for several years, you will rethink your business and make changes. Change is very difficult for some, but is very important. Take it one step at a time, but it is important that you take those steps. It will be easier if you go through the exercises and put your life, first. You'll see it will breathe new life and energy in you.

# Chapter Three - Pillar Two - Vision

Before you lay out the new vision for your business, I want you to **think about your life, first**. Your life and lifestyle are more important than your business, so decide what you want for your life and then design your business to support your life. If you can't articulate how you want your life to be, how can you design your business to support it? Your life is important, so take it seriously and give it the attention it deserves.

My guess is that, when you started your business, you went at it with determination to get the work in front of you done. I'm suggesting you go to work on your life in the same way. Live out the future you see for your life and give it the same importance you've given to your business.

Here are just a few examples of questions you might think about. I'm sure you can think of many more, so don't rush yourself, but think about the answers.

- What do you value most in your life?
- What kind of life or lifestyle do you want to have?
- What do you wish your life to look like day to day?
- How much money will you need to make to live your chosen lifestyle?
- Who do you wish to be and be thought of?
- How does your business fit into your life?
- How will your business serve your life and lifestyle?

Most owners, who started their business by creating a job, gave little thought to their life. They just went to work to make a living. They forgot their life is the most important thing and should be thought about seriously. Your business is not your life, but for many, it's hard to separate the two.

Once you decide what you want for your life and lifestyle, it's time to think about what you want for your business going forward and how it will serve your lifestyle, not the other way around. Always remember, you are not your business.

- What do you want your business to be?
- How will you design it, so it serves your life?
- What do you see in the future for your company?
- How long will it take you to get the business where you want it to be?
- What segment of the construction industry will you serve?
- How big do you want it to be?
- What gross revenues and gross profits will you need to serve your lifestyle?
- When do you want to get it there?
- What kind of special equipment will you need?
- How much capital will it take to get your business where you want it?
- How many people will you need?

You can see many questions need to be answered to take your business in the direction you want it to go. You will undoubtedly change your mind with some and forget to ask others, but at least, you will start with a plan. Write your plan down, so you can articulate it properly. A plan that isn't written down is no plan at all.

Any plan is better than no plan, because you are, at least, looking beyond the work to be done and seeing a bigger picture. You've now taken the first step in building a business that will work without you.

Once you've decided what your life will be and what the business will be to serve that life, you are ready to lay out your objectives. I will get into planning in a later chapter, but for this chapter, let's think about an overall strategy for your business, so it meets your life plan.

**How much money will you need?**

This is one of the first things you need to think about as you plan your business going forward. How much gross revenue will you need to meet your lifestyle? If you've been in business for several years, this isn't that difficult. You know a lot about your numbers, or at least, you should. You will know your gross revenue, your net revenue, your gross profit, and your net profit.

Are you earning enough to live your lifestyle? Have you accumulated assets outside of your income to support your lifestyle during the ups and downs of the construction industry? There's one thing we can all agree on. The construction industry goes in cycles. Not that long ago, the housing bubble burst, causing many companies to shut their doors. I've got a chapter on understanding your numbers later in the book.

**What market segment will you serve?**

If you've been in business for several years, much of this may not apply to you, but it's worth thinking about. Many small companies try to be all things to all people, but that rarely works. The owners I have worked with, who pick an area to become expert, do better than the jack of all trades. There are exceptions to everything.

What business are you in? Are you in the right market for your expertise or do you need to make changes? Is there enough business and profit in your current market? For example, the government market has very low margins. Unless you have a well-tuned construction company and can bring your projects in on budget, this is a tough market to be in. Any prevailing wage job is tough for many contractors, but many went in that direction after the housing crisis hit. Sadly, many of those are now out of business.

Although this is a short chapter, it is one of the most important, because it will lay the foundation for your future in the business going forward. Change is difficult, but if you lay out a good strategy, you'll find you look at your business in a whole new way. You'll find renewed energy and a new outlook going forward.

The next pillar is on planning, so your vision plays an important role in the planning area. Do your homework.

## Chapter Four - Pillar Three – Planning

This section on planning is not like any planning you've done before. It's not a plan to show your bank or your investors. This plan determines how your business will support your lifestyle. It goes like this: life first, business second. Finding the proper balance in this relationship is one of the most important things you can do to improve your life.

This will, undoubtedly, seem very strange and undoable, but believe me, it is doable. Remember the first pillar is **intention** and requires the **commitment** on your part to make it happen. This won't happen overnight, but it will happen if you have a plan and stick to the ultimate goal. Remember, keep the end in sight. What would your ideal business look like? Think like Tom Watson of IBM.

One of my clients recently told me he can finally take a 3-week vacation. He tells his staff he will call in every Wednesday at a certain time. He said it almost hurts his feelings when they tell him everything is fine and he isn't needed. How great is that?

It is important you write things down. Make notes as you go through this chapter, so you can organize it into your plan. A plan not written is not a plan. It is just a collection of thoughts and ideas. You will make changes as you go along, but at least, you will have a plan and an end goal.

**Your ideal lifestyle**

If you could live your life anyway you wanted, how would you do so? Let's assume for this exercise that money was not an issue. You can go overboard and decide you'd like to live like the Kardashian's or some other famous person, but get real about this.

What's most important to you? Go back and review the answers you gave with Pillar Two and your vision. If you didn't put much thought into those questions, do so now. Let's review:

- What do you value most in your life?
- What kind of life or lifestyle do you want to have?
- What do you wish your life to look like day to day?
- How much money will you need to make to live your chosen lifestyle?
- Who do you wish to be and be thought of?
- How does your business fit into your life?
- How will your business serve your life and lifestyle?

Remember we want to design our lifestyle first, and then design the business to support your vision.

How do you want to live your life? What's your dream?

One of my clients organized his business, so he could do more off-road racing. His passion was to race through Baja, CA. Today is June 4, 2016. Guess where he is today? He is participating in the Baja 500 in Mexico. It took a lot of work and practice to get there, but he organized his business, so he could do so.

Another client loves golf and organized his business, so he can play golf 3 times a week with his buddies. Another client loves to fish, so he bought a 40-foot boat and spends much of his day working on the boat, but has his cell phone nearby in case he's needed at work. He keeps his boat in Mission Bay, and his company isn't too far away. One client told me his company is organized, so his only job is to take potential clients to lunch, kiss their rear end, and try to get their business.

None of these owners accomplished these lifestyles overnight, but they had a plan, determined what they needed to do, and got it done. All of them have the checks and balances, so they know how the business is doing, even when they aren't there, personally. They are informed on how the projects are running; they know what their AR and AP are doing, etc. They haven't abdicated responsibility; they've just delegated it with systems that keep them informed.

**How do you want to live your life?** When you started your business, were you planning on working 12 hours a day with unbelievable stress? Probably not, and you don't have to accept that as normal.

Make a list of those things that are important to you. Do you want to spend more time with your family, be home for dinner every night, spend more time with your hobbies, take more vacations? What's your ideal lifestyle? If you can dream it, you can create it if it is important enough.

Determine how much money you have to bring home to live your lifestyle. Are you producing that amount of income? If not, what would you need to do so? Do you have to grow the business more? Is there enough business out there to reach your goal? We'll look at your numbers later in this book, but for now, just look at your current situation. This is a journey you're about to embark on.

**What role do you play in your business?**

- How do you spend your typical day?
- Do you ever come to work with ideas of what you'd like to get done that day and find yourself pulled in too many directions?
- Do you ever try to put systems or procedures in place, but find you don't have time to complete them?
- Do you have half-finished job descriptions lying around?
- Do you have trouble deciding exactly what your job should be and what tasks you should perform?
- How many hours do you work each day?
- How many hours should you be working or how many would you rather work?
- What jobs are you performing that could be done by someone else with proper training?
- How easy is it for you to let go of a job and delegate it to someone else?
- Do you get upset when it isn't done exactly the way you'd have done it?

For the next 30 days, I want you to write down everything you do each day in your business. Don't leave anything out, even what may seem trivial. Keep a list for each day of the week, i.e., Monday, Tuesday, etc.

Remember there are 3 roles in each business. They are a technician, the manager, and an entrepreneur. Beside each task you performed, put a T for technician, M for manager, and E for entrepreneur. When you're doing work in the role of leadership, that is an E. When you're doing work that is tactical, such as working on a project, that is more than likely the role of the technician. If you're managing a project, that is management and gets an M. If you're like most of my clients, you'll be surprised at how much time you spend doing tactical work as a technician. That's part of what we want to work on.

Now, make a list of those things you think only you can do. We all have them, and most of the time, it isn't true. We just haven't replaced ourselves by training someone else to do them. Make a list of those things you like to do. Where are you the most comfortable? This is tough for many owners, so decide how important your goal is.

I've worked with one client off and on for 12 years. I've helped him organize his business, so most of the work can get done without him. He is always home for dinner, spends time with the family, takes vacations, and enjoys his life. When he's at work, though, he still spends most of his day in the field, doing tactical work.

You've heard the old saying, "You can take the boy out of the country, but you can't take the country out of the boy." Well, I took the boy out of the field, but I can't take the field out of the boy. You get what I mean. The important thing is you organize your business, so you can spend your time how you want to. In his case, he likes to spend time in the field, working with his guys.

## The First Steps in Planning

Once you've decided what you want your life to look like and what you want your business to be, it is time to put together your plan. Your plan should be a living thing, not something you put in a drawer or on the shelf to gather dust. Now that you're clear on what you want your life to be, it's time to build the business plan to support your lifestyle.

One common thread runs through most contractors I've worked with over the last 20+ years; it's a lack of planning. A contractor without a plan simply goes to work every day and has a job, not a business. A contractor without a plan is doomed to fail. You wouldn't start a job without a bid or plan, so why would you think you can run a company without a plan?

Four plans are essential to the success of a contractor's business. These are:

1. The Strategic Business Plan
2. The Job Plan or Bid
3. The Completion Plan
4. The Succession Plan

I will go through each of these in some detail.

## The Strategic Business Plan

The Strategic Business Plan is probably one of the most underused and underrated, but most important plans for contractors. This is a plan that should be done before you open your doors. I have found many contractors, who have been in business for 20 and 30 years, have never done a Strategic Business Plan.

Going back to the good old days of 1995 – 2006, all you had to do to make money was to be in business. There was so much business that planning didn't seem as important. Of course, that wasn't true then, and it isn't true after the housing bubble burst and the economy collapsed. Those contractors, who had done basic planning, survived. Many of those, who had done no planning, didn't.

The Strategic Business Plan provides a company with both clarity and purpose. It provides the owner and other decision-makers a clear understanding of where the company is going. It allows the contractor and the management team to make choices that benefit the company's goals. It will eliminate many of the conflicting situations that can arise when managers want to go their own way.

Let me give you examples. Part of my job, initially, is to interview the key managers of a company to get their input on what they see in the company. 80% of the time, when asking what they think the company's goals are, I get several answers or no answer. It's not enough to say our goal is to make a profit. If the management team isn't on the same page, all going in the same direction, how are you going to succeed?

The Strategic Business Plan also provides purpose. Managers in any contracting business must make decisions, based on the goals of the company. The choices they make will affect the outcome of a job and the bottom line results. If there is not a clear understanding and a clear purpose, managers often make decisions, based on their personal feelings. As an example, one Field Superintendent once told me he didn't care how a project was bid; he would do it the way he wanted to. How do you think those projects turned out?

**Strategic Business Planning Components**

There are two basic components to Strategic Business Planning. The first is strategy. Strategy is the framework, which guides those choices that determine the nature and direction of a contractor's business. An analogy might be a fish living in water. Everything the fish does is within the water, where it lives. The water is the framework for the fish. It can do nothing outside of the framework.

Water is to the fish what strategy is to a contractor's business. Strategy is the framework within which everything is done. Strategy then provides and defines opportunities, but puts limits on what can and can't be done. It dictates the possible alternatives available to the business and development of the company.

While the analogy of the fish may seem silly, it makes the point that strategy is an important part of the planning process. It controls the future of a company by limiting which path a company can take. It provides direction for the management team and gets everyone on the same page.

Where strategy is the framework by which alternatives are laid out, planning is the determination of the choices within that framework. Strategy is the "What" of the contractor's business; planning defines the "How." Therefore, planning without strategy is very risky and can cause the failure of the contractor's business. If there is no planning on how the business is to be done, each manager is left to make their own decisions. Without consistency of management, you will have inconsistency of results.

## Mission Statement

The mission statement is the first step to your Strategic Business Plan, because it answers the question, "What I do." It is a statement of your specific intent, purpose, and the reason for your existence. It defines the market or customer needs, the product or service to be provided to meet those needs, your employee goals, and your competitive goal.

## Example Mission Statement

*"XYZ Company is a high-quality distributor and installer of doors and hardware. Our goal is to provide customers with the highest quality finish products, installed in an expert manner, focusing on the needs of each customer, with friendly, energetic enthusiasm. The company finds creative solutions to customer concerns, maintaining flexibility to meet the ever-changing demands of the marketplace.*

*The company prides itself on providing a friendly, family-oriented environment and excellent customer service. Customer satisfaction is the goal of every employee by providing courteous, flexible, high-quality service. Each employee is dedicated to being accessible, responsive, and courteous to their customers. Being centrally located gives the company the opportunity to provide services for a wide variety of customers.*

*The company provides a work environment that is challenging, safe, pleasant, and diverse and will provide employees with opportunities for growth and continued success. Employees are encouraged to think outside the box and inform management of better processes that will help the company and its customers. Employees respond by giving 110% to make sure company goals are met."*

A mission statement can be one sentence, one paragraph, or an entire page. The primary goal is to make a clear statement of what you do.

**Strategic Vision**

This is where you define what you want to be in the future. It's best to do this in three to five year increments. Answer the question, where do you want to be in the next three to five years? If you involve your management team, you will ensure everyone buys in and is on the same page. The decision is ultimately the owner's, but the management team should offer their thoughts. Be as specific as you can with this process.

**Strategic Areas of Focus (Key Processes)**

This is where you determine what you need to do to achieve your goals. What are the processes you need to focus your strategies and resources on to implement your vision and the ultimate mission of the company? These processes will make the difference between success and failure. These are your checkmarks or benchmarks along the way.

**Long-Term Measures and Goals**

This is where you determine how you will measure your progress and whether you are on track or headed in the wrong direction. Long-term measures are standards that describe your status of performance and allow you to compare your plans against your actual progress toward achieving your mission.

Long-term goals are the specific values for each measure to be achieved in a defined time long-term timeframe.

**Long-Term Strategies**

This is where you determine what you need to do to get there. These are planned actions, designed to help you achieve your long-term goals and measures. They address the strategic areas of focus. These may involve major expenditures, such as capital equipment or the purchase of a building, etc.

**Short-Term Measures and Goals**

This is where you establish checkpoints for your short-term goals. They may be similar to the long-term goals, but they differ because their purpose is to measure your progress toward your short-term goals by monitoring the stages of progression.

Where your long-term goals may be three to five years out, your short-term goals may be three to six months out. Both long-term and short-term goals are critical to the overall success of your mission and strategic plan.

**Short-Term Tactics**

This is where you determine what you will do to reach your checkpoints. Think of the short-term checkpoints as stepping stones to your long-term goals.

The best way I can explain this process to you is this:

Suppose you are a finish contractor and you are doing around $6 million dollars in revenue. You haven't been able to grow because everything depends on your oversight. Sound familiar?

Your goal is to grow the business to $10 or $15 million, while maintaining your margins. You know that to do that, you need to make changes with the way you manage, so you need to lay out a strategic plan that will get you to your goal.

In the short-term, you know that to reduce your involvement, you need to have systems and checks and balances that allow you to turn loose of the day to day management of things. One of your short-term goals then must be to develop systems and controls for the field.

You also realize that to grow, you will need to hire and train people with a system that is consistent with high-quality results. You want to hire people and get them up to speed quickly.

Do you get the picture? This is how you set down and begin laying the foundation for your success, both long-term and short-term. Lay out your vision, first, and then build your strategic plan around it.

**The Job Plan or Bid**

The Job Plan or Bid includes everything a contractor must know, have, and do to complete a job and make a profit. Without sound knowledge, the chances of something going wrong is likely. A contractor does his or her best to be the low bidder to get the job, and then panic sets in, wondering if anything was missed in the bid.

You must have a complete understanding of the plan documents and the expectations of the customer, any sub-contractors, the general contractor, and the architect. Don't spare any effort to get clear on what is expected. You need to have a complete understanding of your numbers when putting together the bid. That means understanding your labor burden and your overhead allocation. I've seen more contractors lose their shirt because they either used the wrong numbers or no numbers. Don't let that happen to you. Do you know your breakeven point? Most contractors don't.

As you put the bid together, determine what you need to have. This includes resources, such as money, equipment, manpower, material, and may include a bond. Make sure you have enough money to complete the job and then wait 90 days or more to get paid. This can vary, depending on who you're working for. General contractors have been known to drag their feet in paying their sub-contractors. Having enough money to complete the job, without creating cash flow problems, is essential. It is wise to have a cash flow management system in place.

**The Completion Plan**

Before beginning each job, you should ask yourself, "What do I need to do in order to complete this job on time and on budget?" This is truly where the make or break of a job is determined, if your bid was a good one. This is also where I see the most problems for contractors.

You need to have a clear objective and standards for anyone working on the job for you. You need to have benchmarks for how and when each phase should be done. If you bid a job with so much to be accomplished each day, you need to hold people accountable. If you have the systems in place, including how each phase of the job is to be completed and a Work in Process statement, you will find your jobs running much better.

The key to this is having systems and benchmarks in place for how the job is to be done. I'll get into more of this later, but let me drop a bombshell, here. You can't manage people; you can only manage systems.

More often than not, I see contractors living on **Hopium**. That means bidding a job and then hoping it comes in on-time and on-budget. This is not what you want to do.

If you've done your homework and put together a good plan, you should be able to do Job Costing and determine how the job ran vs. how it was bid. Did you hit your numbers for material, labor, etc.? If not, what went wrong? It's only through a good job costing system you can identify weaknesses. Unfortunately, few contractors actually do job costing. That is a big mistake, because you'll never be able to improve and protect your margins, until you can see what is working and what is not working.

## The Benefits of Planning

By now, you should understand the benefits of doing your homework and planning your business. It will make the difference in whether you have a job or a business. It will make the difference in whether you can run your business, instead of letting the business run you. **It is actually possible to have a contracting business and a life, too.**

Imagine what it would be like to be home for dinner every night and to go to your kid's activities. Imagine what it would be like to have weekends free to spend with the family. I hate to tell you how many divorces I've seen among contractors, because they simply didn't have time for anything, but their business. It need not be that way.

If you've done a good job with the first three plans, you're ready for the fourth important plan.

## Succession Planning – The Ultimate Plan

It may seem odd to discuss retirement in a book about lifestyle. This discussion is about what to do with the business only, but other plans should be made in addition, such as setting up qualified retirement accounts and investing outside your business. Selling your construction company may not be easy, especially if you haven't done a good job of planning.

However, if you've done a good job of planning and building your asset, selling it and retiring is the ultimate end plan. Have you given any thought what you will do with your business, once you've decided to retire? You've worked hard for several years, and if you've done a good job, it's time to reap the rewards of your efforts.

Most contractors haven't given any thought to retiring, and most don't even want to discuss it or think about it. That is a huge mistake, because building an exit strategy or succession plan is a five-year project, at least. There are many things to consider; waiting until the last minute is a big mistake. Let me give you an example.

One contractor I met, several years ago, had sold his business to his employees and assumed they could run the business well enough to pay him off. Two years later, he had to come back and assume control, because the business was failing. When we did a review of the business, we discovered he didn't have systems in place, so the business could run without him being there. He had not done a good job of planning as discussed in the first three plans. Two years later, after we had installed the systems and trained his people, he could retire with more confidence.

When thinking of selling your business to your employees, there are several things to consider. First, can they run the business without your help? Have you done your planning and put the checks and balances in place? Can they qualify for the credit line and bonding needed to continue the business? Is there more than one employee who wants to own the business?

A few years ago, I worked with a plumbing contractor with a great business. He had a good accountant, a good superintendent, and both wanted to own the business. They had talked for several years that the plan was for him to retire, and they would buy the business. When the time came, the accountant and superintendent had no money, couldn't get the line of credit, or the bonding. They had all talked for years about their goal, but they didn't stop to figure out what would be required. There was no plan in place to realize their dream.

There are other reasons to have a succession plan in place, besides retirement. A sudden death or disabling injury can devastate a business. If an owner dies or becomes disabled, without having solid plans in place, what happens to the business? If the business can't run without the owner, what happens to the business? Does the wife step in? Do the kids step in? Does the family have a fire sale and hope to get enough money to pay off the debts?

I worked with a business after the owner died, and the wife tried to assume control. There were no systems in place to run the business, and what she knew could be written on the back of a postage stamp. While there were good people in place, the managers had a hard time accepting her leadership. Fortunately, the lead superintendent worked with her to teach her the business. After we helped install the systems needed, the business steadied out and the business survived. The superintendent and the owner's wife could work well together, and the rest, as they say, is history.

**Summary**

It should be clear that planning is essential. Without it, too many things can go wrong and usually do. If you're going to invest your money and time and assume the risk involved in owning a contracting company, you may as well do it right.

## Chapter Five - Pillar Four – Organize

Over the years, I have met with several contractors, who said they didn't believe in having an organizational chart, job descriptions, or written systems and procedures. They felt it would be too restrictive in how they wanted to run their company. Some of those contractors are successful, and some aren't, but none of them are building equity in their company. Most continue to firefight by fixing anything that can go wrong.

Having an organizational chart with clear lines of authority brings clarity and accountability to your company. Just having it on paper and put away in a binder, without using it, is like not having one. Management requires action and laying out an organizational chart with clear lines of authority and with job descriptions, sometimes called position guides, will bring sanity to a difficult business. Otherwise, you'll be working with chaos, while "the inmates run the asylum."

**Create a Functional Organizational System**

Before you build your organizational system, you need to have done your planning first. If you haven't created your **Strategic Business Plan**, go back and do that first. This will give you the foundation for building a Functional Organizational System.

Successful contractors understand a company can only perform well when there is clarity of purpose, scope, and standards of performance are understood by all employees. That begins with clear lines of authority and accountability at every level. Without that solid foundation, you will see inconsistent results from project to project.

When you begin with a well-thought-out organizational chart and clarity of what each job entails, you can determine who best fits that position. Define the positions first, and then pick the person. Too often, I see companies pick the person first and then try to define the position around the person selected. That's a recipe for disaster.

Lines of authority flow from top down, with the owner establishing company goals and direction, first, with the Strategic Business Plan. It is useful to involve the management team when doing this plan, but the final say goes to the owner.

Responsibility and accountability flow from the bottom up. This means each employee is responsible to their supervisor or manager. Each employee should only have one manager. Sometimes, it is hard to accomplish that with a small company, where everyone is wearing more than one hat, but your goal should be to get to this point. With field operations, an employee may have to report to more than one supervisor over a year's period, but never should there be more than one supervisor on a project. That will cause too much confusion and cause problems with the project.

## Organizational Chart Example

This sample organizational chart is one I did for a small construction firm. It is not meant to be what you would build, but shows the clear lines of authority and responsibility.

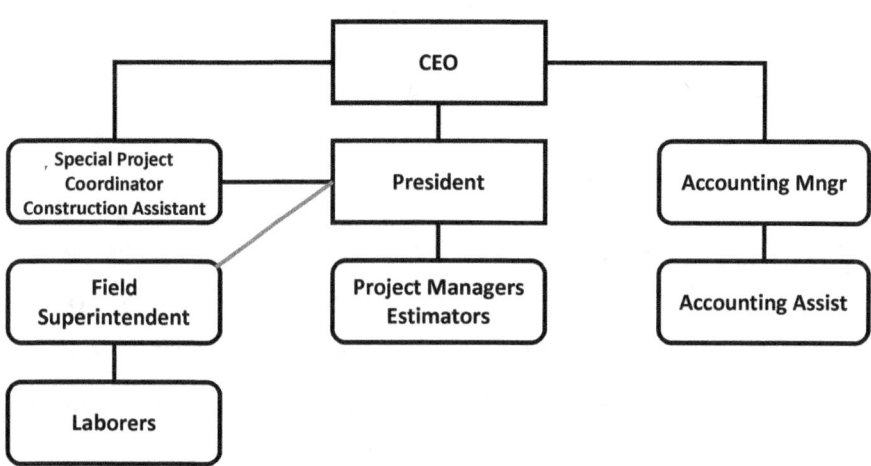

Once the positions are decided upon, it is time to define the position's responsibilities. The clearer you can be, the easier it will be to assign or hire to that position. This is a very important part of building your Functional Organizational System to spend the appropriate amount of time doing this task. If you aren't sure, research it, or work with someone with the experience to help you do it right.

You should define each position as thoroughly as you can. Clearly define the responsibilities of each position and what is expected for each position. As an example, I'm including a job description written for the company shown above, but the names have been changed for privacy. This job description was necessary for this company.

**Note: This first job description is very extensive for this company, but don't throw in the towel. Not all job descriptions must be this extensive. I will give you a form, showing you how to create your own job descriptions, so please don't panic yet.**

**Field Superintendent Job Description**

**1.0 INTRODUCTION**

    1.1    The purpose of this position description is to establish and define the functional role, reporting relationships, duties, authority, responsibilities, job requirements, and measurements of performance of the Field Superintendent.

**2.0 FUNCTIONAL ROLE**

    2.1    The Field Superintendent is responsible to aid in maximizing the profitability of construction jobs by managing to complete work on time and on budget and for the day-to-day operations of the site(s). The Field Superintendent also provides the necessary planning, organization, direction, coordination, and control to meet the established goals of the company.

    2.2    The Field Superintendent must also provide ongoing support and expertise to the field personnel, assisting them in accomplishing the goals, objectives, policies, and procedures for all areas under this position.

## 3.0 REQUIREMENTS

### 3.1 Education:

Required: High School Graduation with trade school.

Preferred: Business or construction related college degree.

### 3.2 Experience:

A minimum of 5 years management experience in construction.

### 3.3 Skill, Knowledge and Abilities:

To use analytical and observation skills, which demonstrates the ability to set a course or direction. Must be able to read and understand blueprints and plans. This position must fulfill the vision and expectations of the President.

### 3.4 Physical:

Body Positions: Standing and sitting

Body Movements: Carrying, use of hands, eyes, arms, and voice.

Must be able to lift up to 100 pounds.

Drug testing: Must pass a drug-screening test, which is given on post hire and on a random basis.

3.5 Mental:

Requires statistical and analytical knowledge using general business math skills. Language requirements are reading, writing, spelling and the ability to communicate clearly on all levels of technical and business levels.

3.6 Working Conditions:

Construction environment. This position may be exposed to very cold or very hot weather conditions and may require walking on uneven or hazardous ground conditions. Will be driving from job sites and have contact with contractors, and sub-contractors.

## 4.0 REPORTING RELATIONSHIPS

4.1 The Field Superintendent reports to the President.

4.2 The following positions reports to the Field Superintendent:

- Laborers report to the Field Superintendent

## 5.0 AUTHORITY

5.1 The Field Superintendent has the authority to operate the areas under his supervision, subjected only to the limitations issued by the President.

5.2 The Field Superintendent can discipline, and recommend the hiring and firing of employees reporting directly to this position to the President.

5.3 With consultation with the President, the Field Superintendent has the right to stop any project if the work is not within the quality standards, expectations of the company, or safety, at which point it will need to be resolved.

**6.0 RESPONSIBILITIES AND DUTIES**

6.1 Review the Job Book with the Project Manager/Estimator for a complete understanding of the project and how the project was estimated.

6.2 Review weekly all job progress from estimate to actual for each project. Keep the Project Manager informed of any issues and next weeks work.

6.3 Plan, coordinate, schedule and control all construction activities by setting job tasks, scheduling crews, assigning responsibilities and providing guidance to employees reporting to him. Arrives on the job promptly as scheduled and always wears identification badges.

6.4 Recognize when a project goes outside of the agreed upon scope of work and notify the Project Manager so that a change order can be written. Be a good steward of the company's money and resources.

6.5 Schedule and request material and supplies needed in advance and in stages or phases and ensure that the material and supplies are available when needed to meet customer requirements. This involves reviewing the drawings and material lists for the project and any other information supplied with the contract.

6.6 Verify the accuracy of packing lists and receipts of any materials and supplies received at the construction sites and <u>transfer all paperwork to the accounting department without delay.</u>

6.7 Coordinate deliveries of materials around equipment and storage units and place in secured area for safe access and ease of control.

6.8 Make every attempt to meet the required project schedules, consistent with high quality output and safe operation of the site activities.

6.9 Maintain construction equipment, vehicles, and tools in good repair. Ensure they are clean, appropriate equipment greased daily, and in good order and recommend changes to meet company quality requirements.

6.10 Use sound budgeting practices and project audits in conjunction with the Estimating department to predict and control cost on a continuing basis for all projects within the estimate for all hard costs and operating expense.

6.11 Directing Construction Operations personnel to meet the objectives of the company:

6.11.1 Manage and supervise the construction operations personnel.

6.11.2 Evaluate the performance of all direct reporting personnel.

6.11.3 Ensure all employees are trained and have the information necessary to do their jobs. This includes the cross training of personnel to enable temporary shifting of job assignments, as required, to ensure the quality and timeliness of project completion.

6.11.4 Ensure that construction operations employees are properly directed, motivated and able to communicate the company mission.

6.11.5 Schedule work review and planning meetings with employees, as necessary, to address work in progress, completion targets, and other vital information needed for smooth and cost-effective work flow.

6.12 Approves daily time cards and assures that they are properly coded and that the proper hours are included for all field personnel reporting to him. Submits time cards according to company policy.

6.13 Maintains, tracks and codes all work related paperwork and submits it to the Project Manager. All properly executed paperwork is submitted to the office within 36 hours of the cost or event. Make sure that all company charges and purchases are properly coded to the proper job and initialed.

6.14    Maintains training certifications needed in order to retain their position.

6.15    Maintaining the job sites as a safe and secure workplace by ensuring that safety programs are followed and insure that personnel operate within sound safety standards.

6.16    Ensure that customer complaints on operations' performance are quickly addressed and resolved.

6.17    Ensure that an adequate back up plan covering the essential functions of the construction operations function is prepared in case the project has to be handed off to someone else.

6.18    Ensure compliance by construction operations personnel with all applicable Federal, State, City, Municipality laws, codes and regulations as required.

Schedules all necessary meetings with appropriate regulatory authorities.

6.19    Ensure all personnel abide by and comply with all rules established by the company.

6.20    Schedules sub-contractors and rental equipment needed for the project...

6.21 Provide appropriate work apparel, tools required to perform your job.

6.22 Maintain, in good condition, original blue line drawings for use in inspections and project close out.

6.23 Prepare and maintain, on a weekly basis, "As-Built drawings and submit them to the Project Manager upon job completion along with a rough closeout package.

6.24 Along with the submission of work in progress reports, daily job log, time sheets, accident reports, turn in other documentation, so accurate accounting records can be completed.

6.25 Inspect job site before, during and after completion of project.

6.26 Keep cell phones and radios on all day and promptly respond to phone messages.

6.27 Keep all lines of communication open between clients, inspectors, and subcontractors by being liaison between them, keep track of all people who come on the site and write in the daily job log.

6.28 Assure that nothing belonging to the company is left on the completed job site.

6.29 Accomplish in-process inspections to assure quality and timeliness of completion.

6.30 Assure the proper maintenance and security of all company assets on the job sites.

6.31 Maintain costs and expenses of operational areas below budget on a daily, weekly, monthly, quarterly and annual basis.

6.32 Ensure safety training is completed each week.

6.33 Provide a new employee orientation and training when appropriate.

6.34 Maintain the discipline of employees to insure quality and quantity of work accomplished.

6.35 To complete any additional assignments as requested by the President.

## 7.0 MEASUREMENTS OF PERFORMANCE

7.1 Project costs and expenses are kept within the estimated costs +/- 5%. Corrective action is taken immediately to change adverse trends. Any variances are supported by documentation and approved by the Project Manager.

7.2 All customer or employee complaints have been or are in the process of being satisfactorily resolved.

7.3 All receipts, invoices, daily logs, etc. are properly coded and turned in to the office as directed.

7.4 Demonstrates good judgment and reasoning when investigating and solving problems and tactfully handle difficult situations.

7.5 Works well with all others in positions of authority.

7.6 Consistently show ability to recognize and deal with priorities.

7.7 Recognizes and performs duties, which need to be performed although not directly assigned.

7.8 Safety is enforced on the job sites and serious accidents or safety violations are kept at zero. All accidents are immediately reported to the Project Manager to be logged in.

7.9 Progress reports reviewed and action taken on all figures out of line.

7.10 All daily reports & safety reports are completed & turned in on time.

7.11 All paperwork is accurate and organized.

7.12 Job sites are inspected prior to beginning to work to assure job problems noted on pre-inspection are handled.

7.13 Satisfactory completion of all projects to the quality expected by the Owners.

## 8.0 ACKNOWLEDGMENTS

This position description does not list all of the duties of the job. You may be asked by the Owners to perform other instructions and duties. You will be evaluated in part based upon your performance of the tasks listed in this position description. I understand management retains the right to change this position description at any time. I also understand this position description is not an employment contract.

_____      _____
Field Superintendent                                                    Date

_____      _____
President                                                                      Date

**Job Description Development Process**

This guide will show you how to develop your job descriptions. You should follow the format, due to the American Disability Association rules. Bypassing these requirements is not a good option.

1.0     INTRODUCTION

        1.1     The purpose of this procedure is to describe the purpose, use, and method of preparing job descriptions. There should be a written job description for each permanent full-time and appropriate part-time position within an organization.

2.0     PURPOSE OF JOB DESCRIPTIONS

        2.1     The purpose is to communicate to employees exactly what is expected of him or her in performing their duties. Knowing what is expected, one can perform to the best of one's abilities.

2.2 The written job description provides a means for open communication between a supervisor and the managers who report to him/her. Discussion of the material in the job description will eliminate possible misunderstanding about what is expected.

2.3 The job description is not meant to be fixed for eternity. Duties, responsibilities, and authorities can change. The Job description should not only be flexible in its wording to accommodate those changes, but the contents should be reviewed, at least, annually to ensure they continue to be appropriate. Input for possible revisions should come from the supervisor and the incumbent of the job under review.

2.4 The job description is also the source document from which all performance and salary reviews stem. Assessment, discussion, and documentation of performance (positive or negative) must be related to the content of the job description and should be specific and objective. The Responsibilities and Duties and Measures of Performance are areas of the job description that, when objectively compared to standards of acceptable performance, help the supervisor and the incumbent get a picture of the level of performance of the latter.

2.5 Job descriptions also assist managers in selecting and hiring the right person for each job under their supervision. They provide the information for hiring new personnel and developing and promoting current staff members into vacant job slots. This requires job descriptions to be prepared, or reviewed and revised for all new management positions before advertising for or interviewing applicants. Hiring managers or promoting employees to new positions, without such document, is somewhat like giving someone a blank check, without describing your needs, to shop for you – money will be spent, but you may not get what you need.

## 3.0 DRAFTING THE JOB DESCRIPTION

3.1 Employee feedback is helpful in developing the guides. They can provide valuable insight into the positions (a touch of reality), and seeking their input will increase their commitment (buy in) to collaborate and perform within the specified guidelines. Comments from employee(s) occupying the position to be described, however, should only to be information for the process. The goa is to follow Functional Organization principles, not tailoring positions to individuals, but the other way around.

3.2 The organization's Positional Organization Chart should not be negotiated or tailored to individuals – whether new or incumbent. If the organizational plan cannot be implemented immediately, an <u>interim</u> plan can be developed, with interim positions and <u>temporarily</u> modified job descriptions. The interim plan, however, must include a method and deadlines for all individuals to adjust their skills or for new people to be brought in to fulfill the original organizational plan – or an acceptable alternative, developed within Functional Organization principles.

3.3 The supervisor of this position will prepare the job description, using the attached form and the following outline:

    3.3.1 <u>Position Title</u>

        3.3.1.1 Indicate the job (i.e., the name of the position).

    3.3.2 <u>Functional Role</u>

        3.3.2.1 In one or two short sentences, explain the position's purpose – and overview of why the job exists, what is supposed to happen as a result of someone functioning in the position.

    3.3.3 <u>Requirements</u>

        3.1.3.1 Detailed descriptions of the education, experience, skill set, and other characteristics/abilities of the individual (including mental, physical and sensory) to have a good probability of success in the position, given conditions imposed by the job.

3.3.4 <u>Reporting Relationship</u>

    3.3.4.1 Indicate to what position this job reports (use the title of the position, <u>not</u> the name of the individual, which is subject to change). Also, show by title, the position(s) reporting directly to the job being described.

3.3.5 <u>Authority</u>

    3.3.5.1 This is the power the position is granted, with prescribed limitations, to take action <u>without</u> the need to obtain prior approval.

3.3.6 <u>Responsibility and Duties</u>

    3.3.6.1 This section is the "what" of the job. Responsibilities are what should be accomplished – the objectives of the job. Duties are specific tasks, required to accomplish those objectives.

3.3.6.2 Both responsibilities and duties are results-oriented, leaving methods to the discretion of the person in the position. Statements in this section begin with the phrase, "Is responsible for…", or define a specific result.

3.3.6.3 It may be difficult to discern whether an expectation is a "duty" or a "responsibility." That semantic description does not matter, however, as long as the individual understands the expectation and s/he is in charge and responsible for its fulfillment.

3.3.7 <u>Measures of Performance</u>

3.3.7.1 These must be specific and, to the extent possible, quantitative measurements to be used in evaluating performance. Examples include: "Monitor and schedule production time, so production costs are within +/- 2% of the original estimate"; "Overtime costs are maintained at less than 5% of the weekly labor costs."

## 4.0 FINALIZING THE JOB DESCRIPTION

4.1 A final draft of the job description must be submitted by the supervisor of the position to his/her own supervisor (usually the General Manager, but not always) for final review and approval.

4.2 After approval, the supervisor can move forward with recruiting and hiring the new manager. If the new Job description is defining the job of an existing employee, s/he and the supervisor must meet to exchange their thoughts on the elements of the document. Successful performance requires a clear understanding of what both parties expect, what it will take to achieve the goals, and how both parties will collaborate to achieve them.

4.3 The meeting is <u>not</u> a negotiation session, but the means to ensure there is a match of interests and a mutual commitment, based on clear understanding of the purpose of the position, its responsibilities, and authorities. If there is not a <u>full agreement</u> on the terms of the position, <u>the employee has no job</u>. If there is a full agreement, both parties should sign the Job description.

4.4 The signature implies no contractual agreement, but an understanding, which includes the employer's right (via the supervisor) to change the job description.

4.5 Once signed by the supervisor and employee, the Job description becomes effective, until changed or modified by the process outlined above.

# Chapter Six - Pillar Five – Building Your Systems

While the first four pillars are important, Pillar Five is where the rubber meets the road. This is where you begin to develop the systems that will become the backbone of your successful construction company. Systems will give you the roadmap to building your construction company so that it is independent of you. This is where you set the standards the company will operate with.

It's important to build systems and procedures for one important reason. You can't manage people; you can only manage systems. While this may seem like an incredible statement, answer this. Have you ever said, or felt like, you just can't get your employees to do things the way you want them to? Another thing I've heard frequently is, "I just can't find good people." Sometimes, that's true, and sometimes, it's not. It depends on your expectations and how well you've hired and shown them what you want.

One plumbing company I worked with, a few years ago, had those exact complaints. He had experienced people, but couldn't get them to do things the way he wanted. After reviewing the company, interviewing the key people, and giving questionnaires to all employees, the problem was clear. There was too much confusion and no clear lines of authority. Good people were all doing their job, as they saw it, with no standards of performance, resulting in chaos.

When you hire experienced people, you expect they know what they're doing and how to do a job from a technical standpoint. I don't mean your systems would tell a plumber, for example, how to change a faucet, etc., but how he or she is to approach each job or project and the steps involved. A plumber with 20 years of experience knows his or her trade. However, they all come with habits and methods they've learned in the past.

If you have a service business, how do you expect your employees to present themselves to the customer? Do you have standards of dress? Do you have certain procedures for how they deal with your customers? Making sure your company presents a consistent, professional presentation can be very important. Examples may be: having a clean truck; having a clean uniform; communicating with the customer; presenting the invoice, etc. Customer service is very important for any service business.

Here's a review for a plumbing company that, obviously, has standards for how their employees are to treat their customers.

*"Daniel was very courteous and knowledgeable. He installed my new faucet and made sure the area was clean when he was finished. Daniel also fixed a couple of dripping faucets and answered questions I had pertaining to my hot water issues. He made some suggestions, but wasn't pushy. I was very satisfied with the services provided."*

## Learn the MacDonald's Way

You can walk into a MacDonald's, anywhere in the world, and know you will get a hamburger and fries that is the same as in any other MacDonald's. The meat is the same quality and weight; the fries are cooked the same anywhere in the world. The operating systems in place are the key to making this work.

When Ray Kroc started MacDonald's, in 1954, and franchised it, he knew it wouldn't work without standards and systems that guided each franchise. He may not have been the first to develop systems like this, but he is one of the pioneers for the restaurant industry. Moreover, these operating systems and controls allow the franchise owners to hire pubescent teenagers, for minimum wage, and still put out a predictable product.

Once he had the operating systems in place, he knew he could duplicate each restaurant with predictable results. You might think of it as a cookie cutter operation or a clone of one restaurant to another. While you may not want to clone your business or franchise it, you may want it to operate with predictable results with each project. To get these results, take a page from Ray Kroc and follow his lead.

**Where do you begin?**

At this point, you should be clear on where you want to go with your company and how you will get there. If you've done your homework, up to this point, by producing your Strategic Business Plan, you know what you want your company to become. By now, you should have laid out your Organizational Chart, so you know the positions and to whom each one reports. Next, are the job descriptions, sometimes called position guides. You may find the need to modify these as you go forward, but that's normal.

Make sure you're clear on what you want from your company, i.e., what's the end result? You will do the same thing with your processes and systems:

- Make a list of the key steps with your business.
- What are the essential processes that link those steps?
- What are the results you want from each step?
- Clearly write a description on how each step is to be done.
- Start with the end in mind. What is the end result you want to achieve?

Think of writing this operating system as a computer program. Put each step into the system, so even I could pick it up and do the task at hand.

Engage your people in the process of developing the systems, after you are clear on the end result you want. Trying to have a consensus is not the proper way to do this. You must first be clear on exactly what you want, and then, let your people help you fill in the steps to get you there.

Be careful not to overdo this and become too restrictive. I've seen owners develop systems that were too restrictive and made it difficult for the business to operate. Don't try to micro manage, but be clear on what you want. **Find a balance**. You want your systems to be thorough, but not restrictive. Once the system is written, give it a chance and be willing to modify it where necessary.

**Sample Operating Procedure for a Project Manager**

The following sample is for a Project Manager I helped my client develop. By putting the steps in writing, there can be no ambiguity. It will make it easier to bring in a new person, when required, and get them quickly up to speed on this function.

The Project Manager receives a file from the Accounting Department, once a contract is signed and accepted by the company. A project number is assigned by the accounting department.

    3.1    Setting up a job file:

        A)    Use a legal file folder and label the folder with the job name, address, and job number.

        B)    Front Insert:

- Take off sheet from the Estimator
- Material selection form
- Job walk sheets – interior and exterior from the Superintendent
- Check list for the Master file required items

        C)    Purchase pouch insert (front)

- Pick Tickets
- Maps
- Jamb and returns/millwork sheets
- PO's (staples with quotes from vendors)

- Material received forms

D) Purchase pouch insert (back)

- Liens
- Invoices (accountant inserts)

E) Back insert

- Quotes (correct one in front, face down are all revised proposals)
- Job estimate sheet
- Signed proposal (signature face front of pile)

3.2 The Superintendent Packet

A) Time standards 1 Super 3 Installers
B) Copy of proposal
C) Map to job site (4)
D) Job Walk Sheet1 Exterior 2 Interior
E) Copy of takeoffs from the Estimator

3.3 After the Superintendent does the job walk, he or she gives the take-off sheet to the Project Manager. The Project Manager converts the quote to a sales order, including labor hours. The sales order must match the dollar amount of the quote.

3.4 Ordering the Job:

A) Create a pick ticket (write PO's next to the material on the ticket and warehouse can check if material is here for delivery.

B) Make copies for the PO's and put them in the front of the purchase pouch.

3.5 After the material is ordered and estimate dates to be received, it is scheduled with the warehouse for delivery. Material received sheets must be attached to the pick ticket for the warehouse to pull the material for delivery. On the date the jambs are to be delivered, it needs to be put on the warehouse schedule the day before we will install. The doors are put on warehouse schedule the day before we will install. The hardware is pulled, and the installer will pick it up. Example (D) means deliver. (P) means pull material for pick up. (PU) means pick up material.

3.6 The Project Manager is responsible for following up with the Site Supervisor to make sure they are ready for the job to begin and then follows the job through to completion.

3.7 When the job is completed, the Project Manager meets with the Superintendent and Estimator to close out the job and determine whether the job made money and to discuss any problems.

While this may seem like a formidable task, it is worthwhile because of the improved results you will get. When you can get predictable results from each task, you have a system that works and provides huge benefits. The work you put in here will pay dividends for years to come and allow you to have a successful business, without giving up the rest of your life.

Pay particular attention to those things that you feel that only you can do. You should develop a system that is thorough and complete so that you can train someone else to do those jobs. Keep in mind, this isn't going to happen overnight, but it is a goal worth pursuing.

# Chapter Seven – Know Your Numbers

It's interesting how many contractors don't fully understand or know all of their numbers, before they submit a job plan or bid. Sometimes, they need a project so badly they throw out a bid and pray. Sometimes, they know their numbers, but bid low anyway and plan to make it up with change orders. Neither practice is sound, so this chapter is intended to show you which numbers are important and how to make sure you're putting the right numbers in your bid, prior to submitting it.

By knowing your numbers and having proper systems in place, you can get away from the term, estimates, and move into the world of promises. I know this seems contrary to the way the construction industry operates, but it can be done if you do your homework. It has to begin with a commitment from top down. In other words, the owner has to make the decision to change, and change isn't easy. The benefits of change, however, are enormous.

**Proof of benefits of change**

Over the last 20+ years, I've received several letters and reviews online from clients. This is what one client had to say, in his own words, taken from his letter.

*Dear John,*

*"I just wanted you to know what a difference the systems and procedures your company installed have made over the past two years. It took a while to get in the groove and to get my staff used to the new procedures, but the proof is in the pudding – our bottom*

line has doubled, and our sales are up 200%, since the systems were installed. You could say the increase in sales is a result of the economy, but without the controls in place, I'm sure our margins would have declined as the volume went up. Just the opposite is happening.

LIFE IS GREAT!!!

I'm sure I'll be calling you again as our business continues to grow."

Best Regards,

Guy H. Evans
Guy Evans, Inc.

When you take the time and make the effort to install the proper planning, systems, and procedures , only good can come from it. You can finally stop firefighting and start building equity in your business, without giving up the rest of your life. Your business isn't your life.

I consider the following numbers and examples to be critical to the foundation of any contractor's business. You need to fully understand your numbers to make a profit with your business.

**Do you know your break-even?**

You should know what your breakeven number is for your company each month, but also know your break-even for each project, before you submit your bid.

A break-even analysis is a useful financial tool for long-range planning. This allows the determination of projected profit or loss and the break-even point when changes are considered from a present day situation.

Break-even analysis can help one identify and analyze the anticipated effect of financial actions, before they are taken. One is working with the relationships between costs, revenue, volume, and profit to develop certain information about one's business.

**Definition of Break-Even**

The Break-even Point is that level of Sales at which all direct costs and other variable costs are covered, all the fixed costs are covered, and the company starts to earn a profit. The breakeven point shows the sales volume at which a company has neither lost money, nor has it made any, either.

**Defining Break-Even Cost Elements**

Fixed Expenses (General & Admin. Expenses) - The expenses of running the business. These costs are stable and unchanging over a wide range of operating levels. They, normally, do not change with the level of sales activity. They are expenses of providing the company's services.

Good examples of fixed costs are Utilities and Administration Salaries. These costs will be the same, regardless of sales volume.

Variable Costs (Direct Costs) - The expenses of providing the company's goods and services.

These costs vary proportionately and directly with the level of business activity. Variable costs would include direct material, direct labor, workman's compensation, other insurances, etc.

Break-even Point - The point where the revenue equals the direct expenses and the fixed costs.

At the break-even point, net profit equals zero.

**Computing Break-Even**

To obtain base statistics for the computation of break-even, the most recent operating statement, profit and loss statement, or the budget projections for the coming year should be used and analyzed. The calculations are taken from the 2003 Profit & Loss Statements of a fictitious company.

The actual or derived statistics of the business must be aligned or accumulated, according to their particular cost category. Next, total all fixed costs.

The next step is to total all variable costs.

The break-even Formula:

$$\text{Break-even (BE)} = \frac{\text{Total Fixed Costs}}{1.0 - (\text{Total Direct Costs} / \text{Total Revenue})}$$

*This formula determines the dollar amount at which business revenues and expenses are the same -- the break-even point.*

Example: Using the data from a sample Profit & Loss Statement

| | |
|---|---|
| Total Revenue (R) | $ 2,989,964 |
| Total Fixed Costs (F) | $ 184,520 |
| Total Direct Costs (DC) | $ 2,767,010 |
| Operating Profit (loss) | $ 40,391 |

**B.E. Point**

184,520 / (1- (2,767,010/2,989,964) =

184,520 / (1 − .9254) = 184,520 / .075

184,520 / .075 = **2,460,266 Break-Even**

**Do you know your overhead allocation number?**

Overhead costs are incidental operating expenses that cannot be specifically identified and charged to a job (examples: Telephone, Office Salaries, Rent, Office Supplies, etc.). The term "overhead" is used interchangeably with "indirect" expenses. Those expenses, identified with a particular job, are "direct" costs, such as Direct Material and Direct Labor.

In the job costing process, overhead must be applied (added to) the direct costs of the specific job by a method, determined to be appropriate for the company. The major reason for doing all the work, defining and allocating overhead, is to assure all jobs completed are anchored on accurate job costs.

It is of equal importance to a company that all overhead costs be covered (absorbed) in its estimating structure, so every overhead item is charged to the corresponding job accurately.

The purpose of this procedure is to present, explain, and detail an acceptable form for identifying and allocating overhead rates, labor burden rates accurately, and assure coverage in estimating.

**Overhead expense accumulation**

It is important overhead formulation and job costing/estimate forms be compatible with company accounting procedures. While it is of great importance to identify, quantify, and allocate these expenses, extreme detail is not always necessary.

Financial records that become part of the income statement to support expense and cost collection are determined, based on accounting needs. Each company must have these records available, before overhead allocation can take place. These records must be current, accurate, and correctly classified on the income statement, deemed pertinent for this company's method of overhead allocation.

For most operations, it is important to decide what portions of these costs are fixed and which are direct. This is especially true if allocations will be predetermined with the budgeting process, rather than calculated from actual, after-the-fact collection of support detail. Classification of expenses, according to their behavior, is of considerable importance in controlling them, developing budgets, calculating predetermined overhead rates, and understanding the effect of overhead on their cost of production.

Once a company is assured that all expenses are captured and classified in as much detail as is important for the specific operation and the income statement produced, overhead allocation to a job may be used.

### Variable and fixed overhead recovery rates

Direct costs for this purpose can be estimated, measured, and billed. Labor, materials, Sub-contracting, and Equipment rentals are components of direct costs.

Overhead expenses are costs and expenses that are difficult or impossible to determine on a job-to-job basis, such as equipment repair, insurance, shop supplies, rent, officers' salaries, etc.

A relationship exists between these components. Based on the period forecast (budget), the total direct costs require a specific amount of overhead expenses. The ratios between total direct costs and overhead are the overhead recovery rates.

This theory demonstrates this relationship is true for the budgeted values and can be extended to each job.

For example, from the attached profit & Loss Statement:

| | |
|---|---|
| Total Direct Labor SC | $647,329 |
| Total Labor Burden SC | $211,789 |
| Total SC G&A Overhead | $221,396* |

*Assumption was made to take 63.5% of the total overhead, since SC was generating about 63.5% of revenue.

Overhead Recovery Rate (O.R.R.) =

$$\text{O.R.R. (BE)} = \frac{\text{Total Overhead Expense SC}}{\text{Total Direct Costs} - \text{Labor \& burden SC}}$$

$$\text{O.R.R. (BE)} = \frac{\$221,396}{\$813,008} = .2723 \text{ or } 27.23\%$$

For every dollar of direct cost, it takes 27.23 cents to cover overhead expenses. The 27.23% is placed on the estimating spreadsheet as Overhead Absorption Rate.

## Do you know your labor burden rate?

### Labor Burden Calculation

From the company's Profit & Loss Statement, the total of direct labor related expenses are totaled then divided by the direct wages. For example:

Payroll Taxes (PT), Workers Comp (WC), Medical (M), Wages (W)

$$\text{Formula} = \frac{PT + WC + M}{W} = \text{Labor Burden Rate}$$

Apply the figures from the Profit & Loss Statement, for example:

$$\frac{66{,}982 + 138{,}577 + 6{,}230}{647{,}329} = \frac{211{,}789}{647{,}329} = .3272 \text{ or } 32.72\% \text{ (Burden Rate)}$$

For every Labor dollar, it takes 32.72 cents to cover labor burden. The 32.72% is placed on the estimating spreadsheet as Labor Burden. The Overhead and labor burden must be figured into and added to each job bid that includes direct labor and materials.

Once all the overhead has been absorbed (breakeven), pricing on bids can be done, as usual, with profit added.

### Weekly Flash Report

A Flash Report is a **"Current Operational Report."** It is a quick overview of the key operating indicators of the company. The purpose of the Flash Report is to provide the Owner and management team with direct insight into the key operating indicators of XYZ Construction on a regular, routine, weekly basis.

The key indicators must tie back to management's performance measurement system.

Charting of the Flash Report indicators over-time will highlight patterns and trends. Unusual fluctuations in these patterns and trends alert you to opportunities or problems, so profitable actions are designed and implemented only on the figures in question.

When a trend is negative, ask the appropriate accountable manager, "Why? What must we do to bring it back in line?" When a trend is positive, ask the manager, "Why? What must we do to keep it positive?"

**Procedure for preparing**

The Accounting & Administration Manager or other designated staff will be responsible for having the Flash Report compiled by 9:00 a.m. every Monday. The previous week's reports are compiled, beginning Monday and ending Saturday. Each section is to be completed, with data furnished by the managers who should have it readily available for their own performance measurement system.

**Complete each section as follows:**

**Financial information** – Describes the financial health of the company.

**Bank Accounts:** Show the checking, saving, and market security beginning balances as of Saturday of the previous week (this information could be obtained from the previous week's flash report - ending balance).

Deposits/Withdrawals: Summarize all deposits/withdrawals made Monday through Saturday.

Ending Balance: Calculate by adding deposits and subtracting withdrawals from beginning balances.

**Line of Credit:** Show the beginning balance of funds, available in the line-of-credit as of Saturday of the previous week.

Uses/Payments: Summarize all uses/payments made Monday through Saturday.

Ending Balance: Calculate by adding payments and subtracting uses from beginning balance.

**Accounts Receivable:** Provides a quick view of the A/R balance and aging. This is key to reducing working capital. A/R should be constantly driven to the lowest possible value.

**Accounts Payable:** Provides a quick view of the A/P balance and aging. It will show how well suppliers are being used to keep down your working capital.

**Sales-** This is your income area.

**Total Number of Proposals Issued:** This will quickly show your current activity rate. If it drops, you should be concerned that billings will also drop over the next 30-60-90-day period.

**Contracts Received:** This is the bookings dollars. The actual billing dollars will vary, up or down, from this amount. Booking dollars are also an indicator of future 30-60-90 day billings.

**Contracts Invoiced:** This is your current income line. It determines your cash flow position and should be closely monitored.

**Contracts On-Hand:** If this number drops, you should be concerned. If the number gets too high, it indicates possible problems in getting out work or will predict problems with meeting the client's schedule.

**Number of Awards Received:** This will quickly show your current activity rate. If it drops, you should be concerned that billings will also drop over the next 30-60-90-day period.

**Success Ratio:** This is your award to bid ratio. If the number drops, you must find out why; what is the competition doing that affects your close rate.

**Note:** Management must monitor the competition and the environment. They must determine what has caused a variance from plan, such as loss of a large contract, aggressive pricing, etc.

**Job progress**

**Total Direct Hours Used:** This targets your return on investment of man-hours. It is critical you constantly compare actual to budget. If the actual hours increase past the budget, then your profits will drop.

**Overtime Hours:** This value must always be controlled. It is one of the leading causes of profit erosion.

**Job Progress:** Each job is tracked by the Production Manager or Operations Manager and shows their ability to eliminate waste and bring in the job at or under the projected budget.

**Analysis**

Monitor the results. Watch for patterns and trends. If a particular Flash Report fits the standard patterns or trends, file it. If some results on a Flash Report deviate from the norm, immediately begin to search for the cause of the deviation and implement corrective action quickly. <u>This is managing by exception.</u> The report will balance three areas of focus, (Accounting, Sales/Estimating, Production/Operations). The week to week fluctuations will allow you the visibility to see where the month is going, before it ends.

This is a living report that can be changed and updated to reflect the current monitoring of anything that affects the income and expense of your company. Review on a regular basis and update as needed.

**The next page shows you a sample flash report form:**

## Sample Flash Report Form

| BANK ACCOUNTS | AMOUNT | SIGNIFICANT JOB ISSUES | |
|---|---|---|---|
| BEGINNING BALANCE | $ - | JOB NAME | ISSUE |
| + DEPOSITS | $ - | | |
| - WITHDRAWLS | $ - | | |
| = ENDING BALANCE | $ - | | |
| LINE OF CREDIT | AMOUNT | | |
| BEGINNING CREDIT | $ - | | |
| - USES | $ - | | |
| + PAYMENTS | $ - | | |
| ENDING CREDIT | $ - | | |
| ACCOUNTS RECEIVABLE | AMOUNT | | |
| BEGINNING BALANCE | $ - | | |
| - RECEIVED | $ - | | |
| + NEW BILLINGS | $ - | | |
| = ENDING BALANCE | $ - | | |
| AGING OF A/R | AMOUNT | | |
| CURRENT | $ - | | |
| 30 DAYS | $ - | | |
| 60 DAYS | $ - | | |
| 90 DAYS AND OVER | $ - | | |
| TOTAL | $ - | | |

| ACCOUNTS PAYABLE | AMOUNT | SIGNIFICANT BUDGET ISSUES | | | | |
|---|---|---|---|---|---|---|
| BEGINNING BALANCE | $ - | JOB NAME | BUDGET | ACTUAL | VARIANCE | REASON |
| - PAYMENTS | $ - | | | | | |
| + NEW INVOICES | $ - | | | | | |
| = ENDING BALANCE | $ - | | | | | |
| AGING OF A/P | AMOUNT | | | | | |
| CURRENT | $ - | | | | | |
| 30 DAYS | $ - | | | | | |
| 60 DAYS | $ - | | | | | |
| 90 DAYS AND OVER | $ - | | | | | |
| TOTAL | $ - | | | | | |

| SALES | | | SCHEDULES NOT MET | | | |
|---|---|---|---|---|---|---|
| | WEEEK | MTD | JOB NAME | SCHED. | PROJ. | REASON |
| CONTRACTS BOOKED | $ - | $ - | | | | |
| BACKLOG OF WORK | 0 | $ - | | | | |
| CONTRACTS BILLED | MONTHLY | $ - | | | | |

| BACKCHARGES | |
|---|---|
| # of Backcharges for the week | |
| $ value of all Backcharges | $0.00 |

COMMENTS:

# Chapter Eight – Performance Management

As you build your Functional Organizational Structure, you want to make sure you get everyone on the same page, with their focus on those things that are most important to the successful operation of your company and your projects.

When you developed your Organizational Chart, you laid out the lines of authority. You then developed job descriptions that spelled out the total scope for each position. Those job descriptions contain everything a position handles. Some would be more important than the other. A job description may have 20 items, but there are 10 that are the most important, which may have a larger impact on overall company performance.

**Performance Management** is built around the 80/20 Rule, which states that 20% of what you do will provide 80% of your results. Likewise, 20% of your employees will give you 80% of your results. By incorporating performance management, with solid performance goals tied to the most important part of your project or work, you will see improved results.

- **Performance Management** encourages higher performance by setting individual performance goals and improves accountability at all levels.

- **Performance Management** recognizes top performers and gives others a clear road map for higher success.

- **Performance Management** can dramatically improve the bottom line, delivering a more focused team of employees.

- **Performance Management** can put the focus on those areas that are most important and need improvement.
- **Performance Management** can improve bid success by focusing on bid building, rather than busy bidding.
- **Performance Management** gives your other managers the tools to motivate employees toward higher levels of production in a positive manner.
- **Performance Management** takes the pressure off of the owner, giving the owner more time to work **on** the business instead of **in** the business.

**Example:**

The first part of this example lays out the job description, and the second part lays out the actual performance goals and measurements. This is an example of how these work together to get what you want from your employees.

**RESPONSIBILITIES AND DUTIES**

To accomplish the duties of the Field Superintendent, the following duties must be accomplished:

- Complete installation schedule daily for all installers & foremen.
- Assure the correct materials are installed at each job, matching the Material Specifications sheet for that job.
- Provide all installers with installation time standards for each job.
- Monitor job progress in relation to time standards for all jobs.

- Provide for the training of new installers, and evaluate the results of this training 14 days, 30 days and 60 days after training begins.
- Review each job with installers before beginning to ensure correct installation procedures are followed.
- Contact Field Foremen daily for reports on progress and material requisition requirements.
- Contact Project Managers by 1:00 PM daily to request materials for delivery/pick up the following morning.
- Meet with Project Manager daily to review job schedules, customer service appointments, and delivery/pick up schedules.
- Assure all installations meet or exceed company standards for materials & workmanship.

Controls all aspects of the job by continual supervision of Field Foremen and installers at the job.

Keep the Project Manager informed of any changes at the site not reflected in the contract.

Ensure all safety policies are followed. Take steps to immediately correct any safety infractions. Conduct bi-monthly safety meetings with all installers.

Prepare all reports required by the General Manager, pertaining to jobsite information.

Properly control installation quality and efficiency.

Direct and implement an effective training program for installation personnel in all phases of finish carpentry and quality control.

Maintain communication with on-site supervisors to insure proper scheduling and appropriate jobsite conditions.

Verify the start and finish times for all installers, verify and sign all time cards, and assure all job and task codes provided are correct.

Provide necessary reports on a daily, weekly or other timely basis used by the project manager, sales, or the accounting department to assist in the efficient operation of the company.

Attend meetings as directed by the General Manager.

Monitor all jobsite materials to minimize waste and shrinkage. Inform Project Managers of any overages available for immediate pick-up.

Evaluate the performance of personnel reporting directly to this position on a semi-annual basis.

Perform any other duties as directed by the General Manager.

**MEASUREMENTS OF PERFORMANCE**

Supervision of installation jobs has resulted in all activities being accomplished in a safe, efficient manner, and in accordance with the directives of the General Manager.

Controls all aspects of the jobs by continual supervision of the Field Foreman and installers, thereby, minimizing mistakes and cost overruns by meeting the time standards of the jobs.

Works well with the Project Manager and keeps them informed of changes or problems on each job.

Ensures all safety policies are followed, conducts bi-weekly safety meetings with all Installers, and takes measures immediately to correct safety violations.

Employee performance evaluations have been accomplished on personnel reporting directly to this position.

Directs and implements an affective training program for installation personnel in all phases of finish carpentry and quality control.

Maintains good communication with on-site supervisors to ensure proper scheduling and appropriate jobsite conditions.

Loss of material has been kept to a minimum due to jobsite management. Notifies the Project Manager of any overages available for immediate pick-up.

Verifies the start and finish times for all installers, verifies and signs all time Cards, and assures all job and task codes provided are correct.

Provides necessary reports on a daily, weekly, or other timely basis, used by the project manager, sales, or the accounting department to assist in the efficient operation of the company.

**As you pull this together, you want to make sure you are clear on your expectations and on how your employee will be evaluated. The following is an example of an evaluation form.**

**Field Superintendent Evaluation Form:**

EMPLOYEE _____

EVALUATOR _____

RATING _____

PREVIOUS RATING _____

REVIEWED BY _____

DATE _____

LENGTH IN CURRENT JOB_____

**RATING:**

**1 - SUBSTANDARD**

**2 - MARGINAL**

**3 - AVERAGE**

**4 - COMMENDABLE**

**5 - OUTSTANDING**

# Employee Effectiveness

| Employee Rating | Manager Rating | (Rate on 1-5 scale: 5 = Outstanding 1 = Substandard |
|---|---|---|
| | | **Supervision** – Supervision of installation jobs have resulted in all activities being accomplished in a safe, efficient manner, and in accordance with the directives of the General Manager. |
| | | **Job Standards** – Controls all aspects of the jobs by continual supervision of the Field Foreman and installers, thereby minimizing mistakes and cost overruns by meeting the time standards of the jobs. |
| | | **Cooperation** – Works well with the Project Manager and keeps them informed of changes or problems on each job. |
| | | **Reporting** – Provides necessary reports on a daily, weekly, or other timely basis, used by the Project Manager, sales, or accounting department to assist in the efficient operation of the company. |
| | | **Employee Reviews** – Employee performance evaluations have been accomplished on personnel reporting directly to this position. |
| | | **Safety** – Ensures all safety policies are followed; conducts bi-monthly safety meetings with all Foremen, Installers and takes measures immediately to correct safety violations. |
| | | **Problem Solving** – Resolves problems before reaching Management. Any unresolved problems were presented with suggested solutions. |
| | | **Employee Morale** – Subordinates are supervised in such a manner that employee morale and productivity is maintained at the highest possible level. |
| | | **Communication** – Maintains good communication with on-site supervisors to ensure proper scheduling and appropriate jobsite conditions. |
| | | **Material** – Loss of material has been kept to a minimum due to jobsite management. Notifies the Project Manager of any overages available for immediate pick-up. |
| | | **Special Projects** – Handles all special projects assigned by Management in an expeditious and efficient manner with proper documentation. |
| | | **Job Verification** – Verifies the start and finish times for all installers, verifies and signs all time cards, and assures all job and task codes provided are correct. |
| | | **Customer Satisfaction** – Customer satisfaction levels are consistently high, and customer disputes are handled to the satisfaction of the customer. |
| | | **Training** – Directs and implements an effective training program for installation personnel in all phases of finish carpentry and quality control. |
| | | **Commitment** – Demonstrates desire to support the success of the team at the expense of personal gain. Is willing to sacrifice *personal desires* for success of the team. Makes a positive, recognizable contribution to the company. |
| | | **Overall Rating of Effectiveness** |

## Getting Started

As a special offer I have created a step by step program that includes templates and coaching that will help you transform your company into the **Ideal Construction Company** that will provide the **Ideal Lifestyle** of your dreams. You truly can have a successful construction company without giving up the rest of your life.

**Go to http://constructionownerlifestyle.info to learn more.**

www.ingramcontent.com/pod-product-compliance
Lightning Source LLC
Chambersburg PA
CBHW071409220526
45469CB00004B/1216